to _____

from _____

the time chamber

10 9 8 7 6 5

Ebury Press, an imprint of Ebury Publishing,
20 Vauxhall Bridge Road,
London, SW1V 2SA

Ebury Press is part of the Penguin Random House group of companies
whose addresses can be found at global.penguinrandomhouse.com

Penguin
Random House
UK

First published in UK by Ebury Press in 2015.
Originally published in Korea by The Business Books and Co., Ltd.,
in 2015. Copyright © Song Ji-Hye (Daria Song).
Translated from Korean by Min Jung Jo.

www.eburypublishing.co.uk

A CIP catalogue record for this book is available from the British Library

ISBN: 978 1 78503 210 3

Design by Margaux Keres

Printed and bound in India by Replika Press Pvt. Ltd.

Penguin Random House is committed to a sustainable future for our
business, our readers and our planet. This book is made from Forest
Stewardship Council® certified paper.

DARIA SONG

A magical story
and colouring book

the time chamber

EBURY PRESS

The red-haired fairy who lived inside the cuckoo
clock was feeling restless. One day, while out in
her rowboat, she began to daydream about the
world outside of her beautiful time garden.

'What does the world outside of the clock look
like?' she wondered.

The red-haired fairy decided to visit the little girl's room
just outside the cuckoo clock. She would bring the girl magical
and mysterious gifts that would turn her ordinary world
into a fantastical playground.

She packed her finest treasures: a magic brush, keys to the time
chamber and the golden clock tower, a time tape measure,
a potion, a starlight candle and a pair of opera glasses.

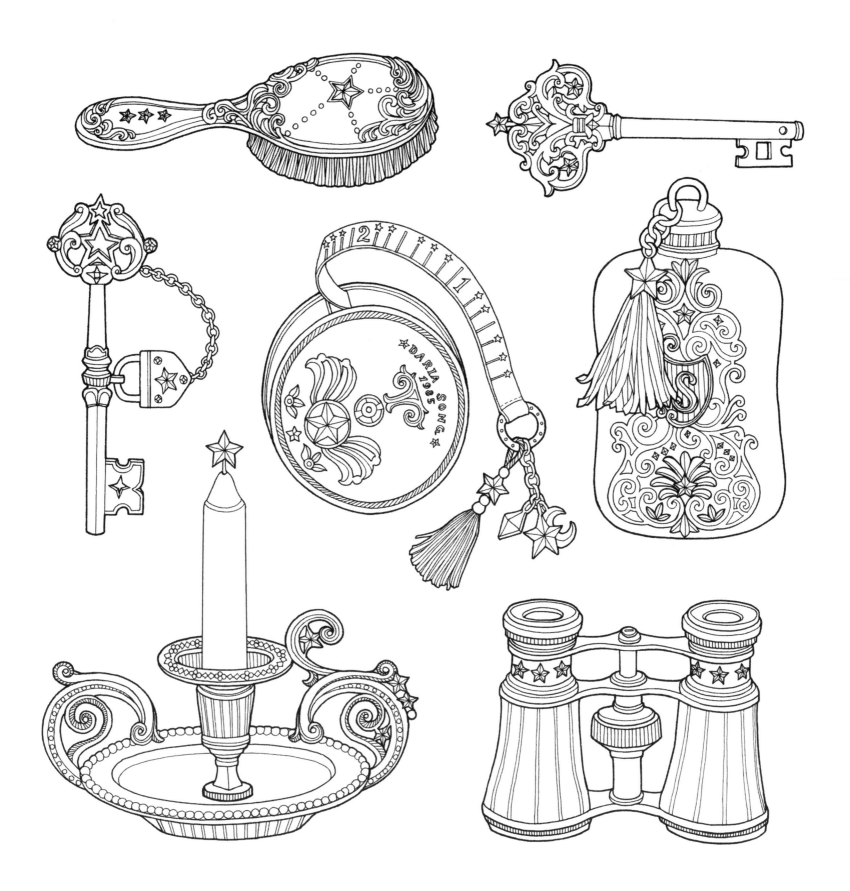

She also brought an owl-feather pen, a
star-scented spray, a dancing fan, a starlight
lantern and a teleport mirror.

After the little girl went to bed,
the fairy stepped out of the door
and swung down the clock's chain.

The fairy discovered a land of treasures
beneath the little girl's bed.

Everything in the girl's world seemed so
enormous and marvellous to the tiny fairy.

Whatever the fairy touched, no matter how
mundane, turned into something beautiful
and mysterious.

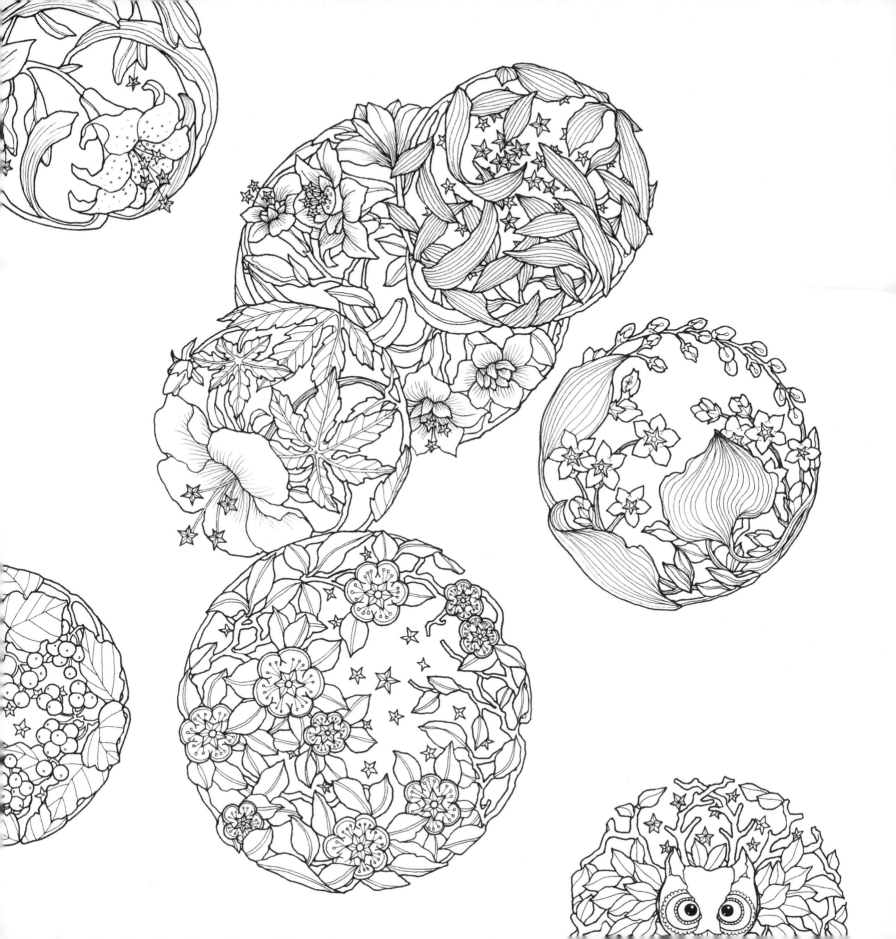

Through her opera glasses, the fairy saw . . .

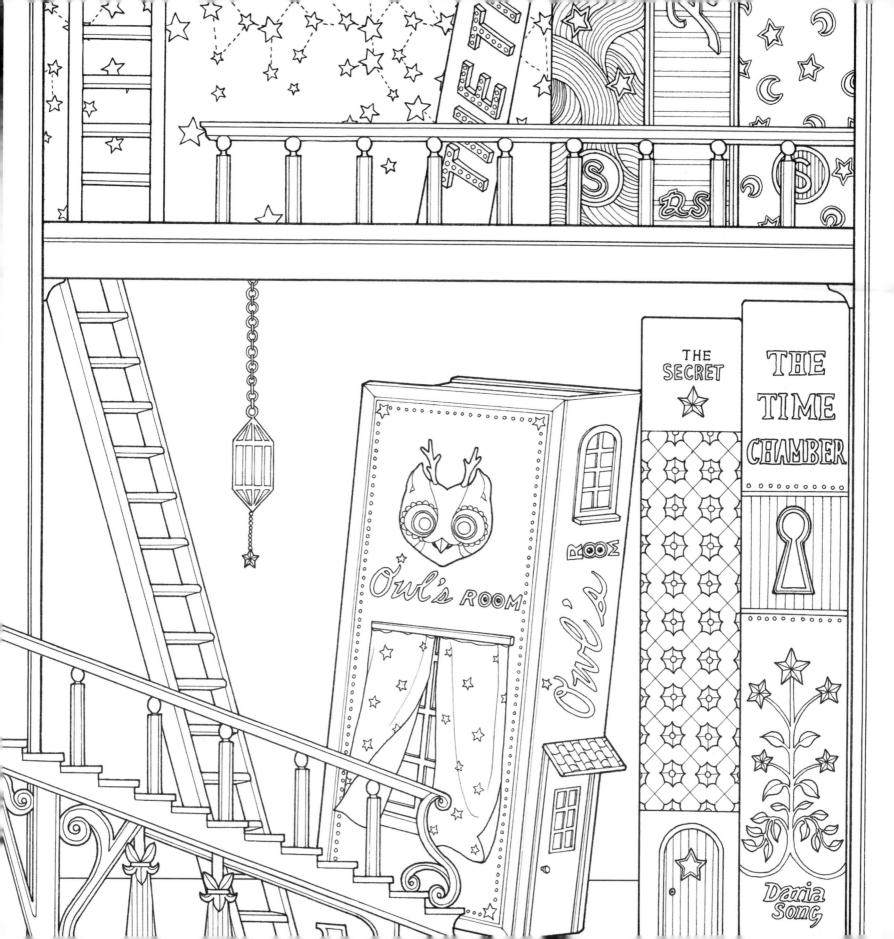

IT'S ALWAYS TEA TIME

The Time Chamber

Worn out from her explorations,
the fairy dropped off to sleep
without even realizing it.

Cuckoo, cuckoo . . . cuckoo.

When the morning chime of the cuckoo clock woke the little girl up, the fairy scurried into a hidden nook.

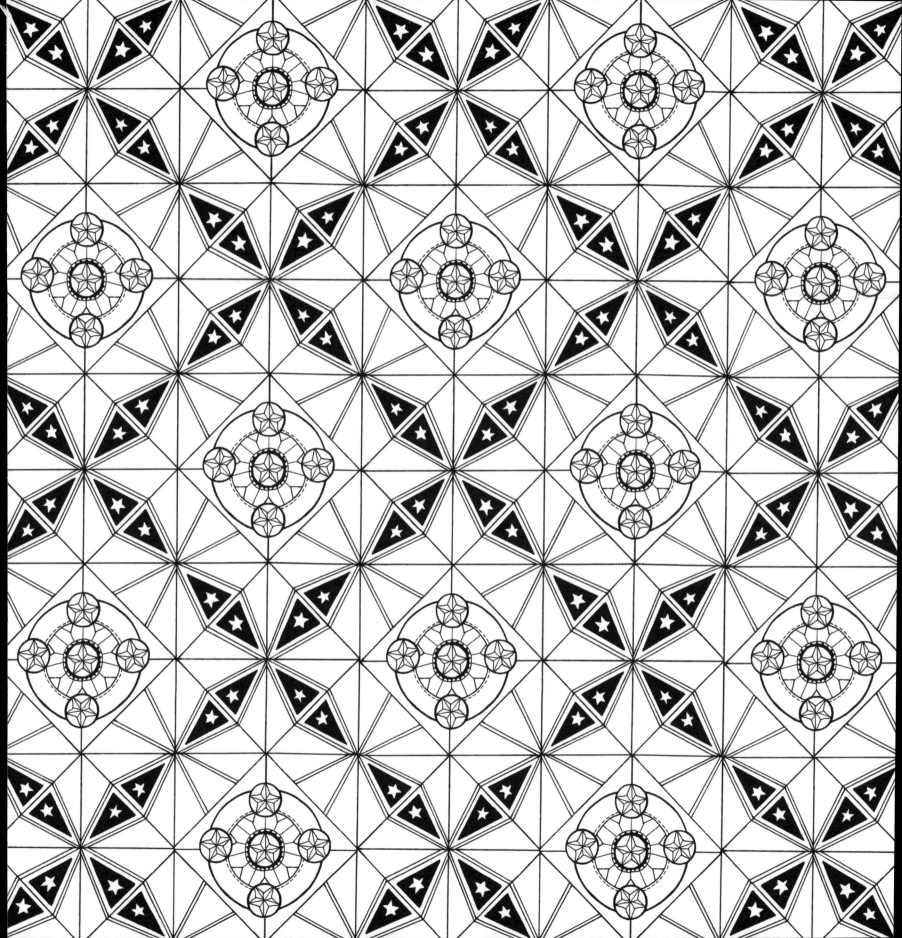

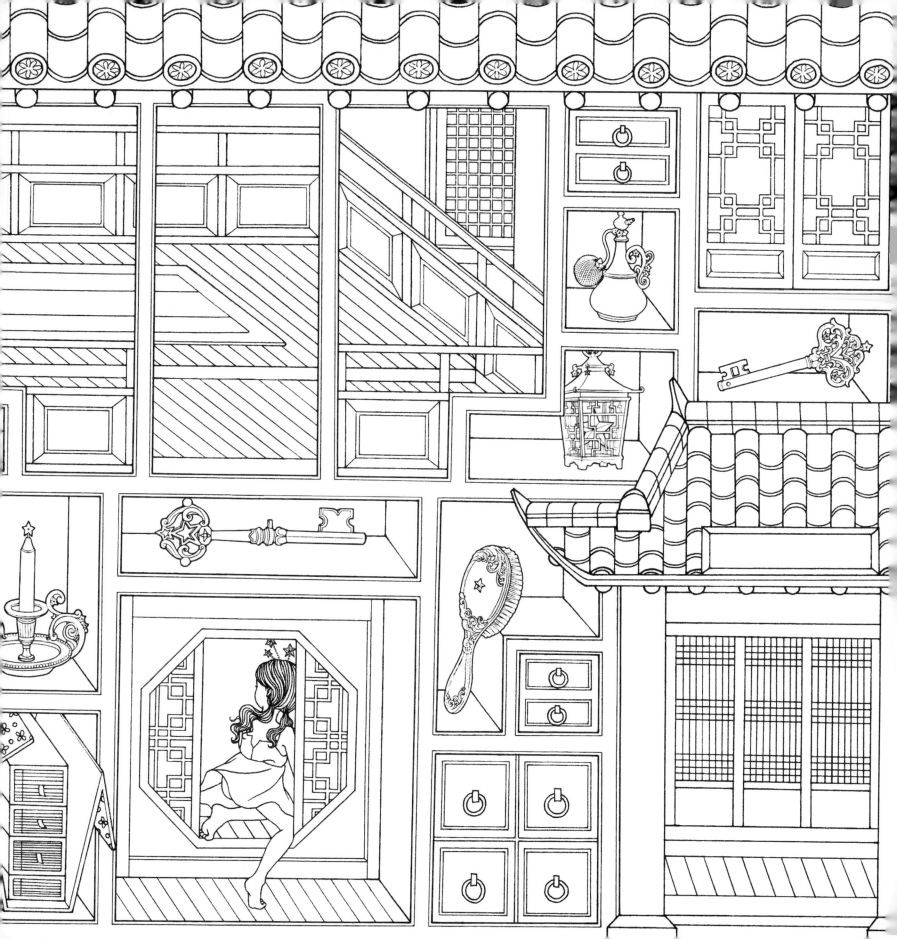

'Good-bye,' the tiny fairy whispered.

Then she climbed back into the clock
and returned to the time garden, waiting
for the day the girl would come and see
her again.

Visual Index and
Hidden Treasure Key

Leaving the Time Garden

Fairy's Treasure List 1

Fairy's Treasure List 2

Coming Out of the Clock

Magical Clock Gears

The Midnight Bedroom

The Mysterious Cabinet and the Clock (Owl-Feather Pen)

Curtains

Cabinet Tram

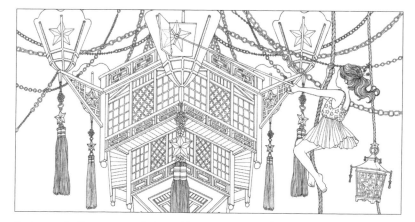

Lighting the Lanterns with Stars (Starlight Lantern)

Starlight Chandelier (Starlight Candle)

Climbing the Starry Fence

Berry Picking in the Flower Vase

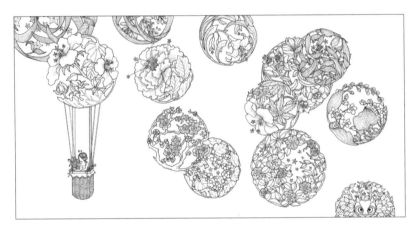

Flowery Air Balloon

Through the Opera Glasses (Opera Glasses)

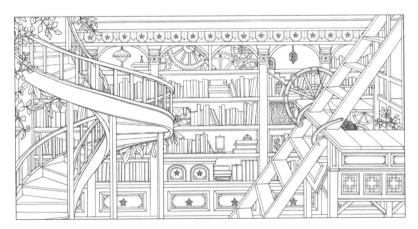

Something Strange in the Library

Library Jungle

The Bookshelter

Secret Key (Key to the Time Chamber)

Key and Ornamental Toys (Key to the Golden Clock Tower)

Mirror on the Wall

Blue Willow Pattern

It's Always Tea Time

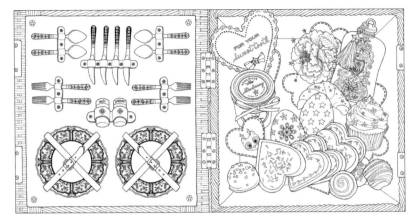

For Your Sweet Tooth (Potion)

Star Scents in the Mysterious Workroom (Star-Scented Spray)

Dancing on the Thread (Dancing Fan)

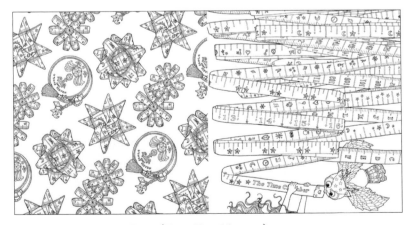

How Do You Measure Time (Time Tape Measure)

Flying Back Asleep

Window **Frame** Puzzle

The Girl with Stardust in Her Hair (Magic Brush)

The Time **Ch**amber Collection

Going Back to the Time Garden

Star Spla**sh**ing Clock

Good-Bye

the time chamber